MW01104816

Praise for Yuyutsu RD Sharma's works

Each poem is a delight in itself, a discovery, a new turn of phrase, a new sensation, a world of sound and light, and visions all colliding against each other to provide an unexpected and haunting experience.
David Clark in *Exiled Ink*, London

Yuyutsu RD lives close to Everest. His poetry climbs mountains, swims in rivers and paints the falling leaves in copper. This tango with nature also occurs when Yuyutsu RD closes the window for a moment...
Ronny Someck in *Iton77*, Tel Aviv

The poems... are shining jewels of passion, energy and splendid craft, redolent with vivid, dreamlike visual imagery, strengthened by realistic observation and powered by strong male eroticism. His is an unabashed return to the male gaze that is refreshing and solemn by turns, reminding one of the stirring sounds of rolling drums and beating rain...
Sucheta Das Gupta in *The Himalayan Times*, Kathmandu

A fiercely sublime poet ...the book confirms an enormous talent, as well as purity of purpose with which he approaches his calling. Lines jump out, burning themselves into your consciousness.
Eddie Woods in *Amsterdam Weekly*

With this buoyantly audacious work, Yuyutsu RD should be assured of his place in the canon of Asian poetry.
In this new volume he conveys the people and places, the flora and fauna of the Annapurna area of Nepal with an exhilaratingly fresh vision. It is poetry where pastoral elegy becomes fused with magic realism; where earthy common-sense mysticism becomes interlaced with a lush sexuality. The book is a voluptuous and loving evocation of Nepal and I admire its dramatic intensity.
Cathal O Searcaigh, Ireland

Yuyutsu RD Sharma has his feet firmly planted on the ground. His poetry is rooted in its landscape and environment and thereby gains its strength. He has also served the muse assiduously over the decades and small wonder that she has rewarded him.
— **Keki N. Daruwala**, *New Delhi*

Yuyutsu RD Sharma's poetry runs clear, tender, and passionate with a rage that often erupts volcanic in the face of the cruelty, despair, and injustice that saddles the disenfranchised poor of the earth. Poems powerful and devastating, yet gentle as flower petals wafting to earth in a summer breeze.
Michael Annis, senior editor, *Howling Dog Press*, Colorado

"Something is always happening in Yuyutsu's poetry. Like some burning concern for truth, something that, I think, a poem should do. For this, we owe Yuyutsu much.
— **Jayanta Mahapatra**, Cuttack, India

Yuyutsu's poetry touches on concerns of global matters, acknowledging that we can never with violence create a Utopia or "construct a gorgeous pagoda from/furious flames/and whistling winds ... Such lines capture for me the futility of the Iraq War, which I refuse to dignify with its official title, even more euphemistic and tainted with doublethink than earlier misadventures. We can't build even a humble pagoda from furious flames and whistling winds.
— **David Ray**, The United States of America

"Yuyutsu R.D. brings to the Indian readers a distinct flavor of the Nepalese landscape and culture, in a sequence of poems that pulsate with needle-sharp images—Equally sensitive is his language that, scrupulously avoids stilted diction-words or phrases. His writing is so densely imagistic that he holds reader's attention all the way through. Behind plethora of packed images is a genuine concern for the human predicament—the trials and tribulations of the destitute everywhere. Hunger is the theme that runs as an under current-hunger that gnaws into the vitals of both humans and animals."
—**Shiv K. Kumar** in *The Hindustan Times*

Yuyutsu has a good eye and a good ear:
The rain stopped in the jungle.
The cicada stopped its chirr.
To have an ear for a sudden silence in unique.
—*The Hindustan Times*

"Yuyutsu's poetry has long been a part of the Nepalese consciousness: we use his more aphoristic lines as a paradigm of contemporary Nepali political and social changes."
—**Sharad Pradhan** in *The Kathmandu Post*

"It is an agony ride through the darkness of modern times. The symbols are powerful and disturbing, the metaphors violent. The female Yeti becomes as icon for man's sexual angst... This collection marks an important phase in the poet's evolution, revealing a more mature poet in terms of symbol, diction and style., 'Hitting notes of a secret language of lust', Yuyutsu has made his poetic presence felt."
—*The Observer*

This is what **Asiaweek** has to say of **Yuyutsu's translations of Nepali poetry**:
'... magnificent achievement evoking lives of Nepalese peasants while remaining highly readable... The reader will come away breathless from these short, wonderfully concentrated poems'

These vivid and readable translations show the poets coming to terms both with political development and with the influence of Western modernism in literature.
— Allen W. Thrasher,
Library of Congress, Washington DC

Nirala Series

ANNAPURNA POEMS

Recipient of fellowships and grants from The Rockefeller Foundation, Ireland Literature Exchange, The Institute for the Translation of Hebrew Literature and The Foundation for the Production and Translation of Dutch Literature, **Yuyutsu RD Sharma** is a distinguished poet and translator. He has published seven poetry collections, including, *Annapurna Poems*, (Nirala, 2008) *www.WayToEverest.de: A photographic and Poetic Journey to the Foot of Everest*, (Epsilonmedia, Germany, 2006) with German photographer Andreas Stimm and recently a translation of Irish poet Cathal O' Searcaigh poetry in Nepali in a bilingual collection entitled, *Kathmandu: Poems: Selected and New, 2006.* He has translated and edited several anthologies of contemporary Nepali poetry in English and launched a literary movement, *Kathya Kayakalpa* (Content Metamorphosis) in Nepali poetry.

Widely traveled author, he has read his works at several prestigious places including Poetry Café, London, Seamus Heaney Centre for Poetry, Belfast, Western Writers' Centre, Galway, WB Yeats' Centre, Sligo, Gustav Stressemann Institute, Bonn, Irish Writers' Centre, Dublin, The Guardian Newsroom, London, Arnofini, Bristol, Borders, London, Royal Society of Dramatic Arts, London, Gunter Grass House, Bremen, GTZ, Kathmandu, Ruigoord, Amsterdam, Nehru Centre, London, Frankfurt Book Fair, Frankfurt, Indian International Centre, New Delhi, and Villa Serbelloni, Italy. He has held workshop in creative writing and translation at Queen's University, Belfast, and South Asian Institute, Heidelberg University, Germany.

His works have appeared in *Poetry Review, Chanrdrabhaga, Sodobnost, Amsterdam Weekly, Indian Literature, Irish Pages, Omega, Howling Dog Press, Exiled Ink, Iton77, Little Magazine, The Telegraph, Indian Express* and *Asiaweek.*

Born at Nakodar, Punjab and educated at Baring Union Christian College, Batala and later at Rajasthan University, Jaipur, Yuyutsu remained active in the literary circles of Rajasthan and acted in plays by Shakespeare, Bertolt Brecht, Harold Pinter, and Edward Albee. Later he taught at various campuses of Punjab University, and Tribhuwan University, Kathmandu.

The Library of Congress has nominated his book of Nepali translations entitled, *Roaring Recitals; Five Nepali Poets* as Best Book of the Year 2001 from Asia under the Program, *A World of Books International Perspectives.*

Yuyutsu's own work has been translated into German, French, Italian, Slovenian, Gaelic, Hebrew, Spanish and Dutch. He edits *Pratik, A Magazine of Contemporary Writing* and contributes literary columns to Nepal's leading daily, *The Himalayan Times* and *Newsfront Weekly*. He has completed a translation of Hebrew poet Ronny Someck and his first novel. He is working on his manuscript of Euro Poems.

More: www.yuyutsu.de

NIRALA ◢ SERIES

Annapurna Poems

Yuyutsu RD Sharma

Poems New & Collected

For Pamela,
an invitation to the Himalayas

Yuyutsu RD Sharma

www.yuyutsu.de

◢
Nirala

Nirala Publications
G.P.O. Box 7004
Daryaganj, New Delhi-110002
niralabooks@yahoo.co.in
niralapublications.com

First Edition 2008

ISBN-81-8250-040-0

Cover Photo: Andreas Stimm

Cover Design: Vimal/Shakti

Printed at
H.S. Offset Printers
New Delhi-110002

Preface

Annapurna Poems

A Story

Fragile my eyeglasses
fragile and foreign
I take them off;
There's a speck of a scar in them.
On the mule path
I take them off
to face the green
stretch of mountains
beneath the saddle of Annapurnas.
From the balcony
of a clay plastered hut, I see
a Sun rise in the clear sky of my life.

Spring, 2002

I don't think I can write a line like the above any more. For the last few years, I have not been able to go to the Annapurnas. I don't think I can complete the poems and books I started and left unfinished years ago.

When the night falls, I dream of those mule paths in the dense pine and fir forests. I hear again the faint sound of crystalline brooks as I climb the flagstone steps of steep hillside paths that lead to the land of Gods.

Only in my dreams can I travel the lonely path from Ghorepane to Tadapani and get lost in the leech-greasy forests.

Last month, my Irish poet friend, Cathal O' Searcaigh came on his annual visit. He said, this time, he could take only a one-day-trek. Cathal could not go beyond Ulleri. He politely said, "I didn't have much time."

Yet I know what could have happened. For last few years, the Annapurnas has come under the grip of the Maoist Insurgents. Their possible confrontation with the Army and a traveler being trapped in the crossfire become very frightening as one plans a trip to the region.

Two years ago as I visited the area people in the area seemed in high spirits. Then "No police, no Maoists" theory was a great relief. I moved freely with my German friend Ida Zeller who took me to *Little Paradise Lodge* on the top of Kimrong Danda that one can view from Gandrung village.

She walked alone for two hours alone in the dense forest in the dark. I do not think at this moment Ida could take such a long evening walk. Nor can I dare to go to the top of the hill and sleep peacefully as a lonely, and only, guest in the wilderness.

My 'affair' with the Annapurnas began years ago. About a decade ago, when I resolved to quit my teaching stint at the Tribhuwan University to opt for a freelance creative writer's career, I had time on my fingers.

One fine morning I moved out of the gossip circles of the Kathmandu Valley and made a trip to Pokhara. I stayed in a small lodge managed by a few young Pokhara boys in partnership. They also organized trekking tours and even escorted tourists to the Annapurna regions.

Staying at the lodge, I came under the spell of these young people who induced me to this world of sunlight and snow. I saw them discussing the details of their treks and exploits of the trekking history. Their travels seemed so strange, full of adventure and romance. They talked of trekkers, strange and sane, the Nepalese ethnicities, the porters from all castes and creeds, the pirates from the eastern and western regions, the thrill and thefts on the trail, the lure, and loss of life and the stories of young lonely woman and murderous drunkards they met on the trail.

To me they were a great repository of the Himalayan lore. They had traveled from very tender age and build up a plump silo of the facts and fiction from the area. They talked of the region with acute accuracy, knew of the hazards and hardships of mountain life as they knew of the local shamans and mysterious Yeti.

Were they talking of the same Nepal where I lived? I wondered and followed their narratives. They were trekking guides and knew Annapurnas very intimately. They knew each inch of the area and unlike the pompous scholars on the subject, they approached the mountains with respect, passion, and audacity. They had traveled with hundreds of visitors and had strangely educated themselves through their experiences with all the nationalities of the Western world.

Awesome details of their amazing stories one day made me store up my belongings in the luggage room of the lodge and rent out a backpack and some warm clothes. Initially, they urged me to take up a two-day teahouse trek to Gandrung.

But I had already fallen in love with the Lake Fewa and didn't have a heart to leave. Virtually scared of the hazard of mountain trekking and just out of comfortable campus circus circles, very reluctantly after a weeklong tinkering with the idea of going all alone in the mountains, I took up a teahouse trek that in due course ended up at Base camp.

Interestingly, Annapurnas have become my lifetime's commitment and I've been on all major mule paths of the region. It has become a practice to visit the area twice a year. I have carried the exceptional mountain world in my heart throughout my visits in Europe and India.

Known all over the world for their magnificent daggers of snow, the Annapurnas and the colorful people in its landscape I have been aspiring to evoke in my writings. A decade ago, I had found a mission, a mission to survive. I could live on for the rest of my life with a purpose. I had found I could at last breathe.

Now with the rise of insurgency and the possible fear of violence due to military confrontation, I haven't been able to visit Annapurnas. The same boys from the Lakeside, who painstakingly convinced me to move into a *real* world, 'a real Nepal' as they then claimed, now brush aside the idea of even a brief trek as futile and risky.

"What there Dai? Stick around Pokhara. We can go across the Lake and take a brief trek or enjoy a full moon party there"

Gandrung, Ghorepani, Tadapani, Tatopani, Chrumung, the white rivers, the forests of rhododendrons, the mules that went up and down the Tibetan salt routes, the fat cockerels that greeted you on the way, the birds—everything has become a thing of past.

Gandrung has turned into a ghost town. The Maoists closed Annapurna Conservation Area Project (ACAP) office. In addition, the Maoist cadres started charging extra entry fee along the ACAP permit in the Annapurnas areas.

Double window system was very vague and led to lot of confusion. ACAP has been considered the most successful NGO under King Mahendra Trust for Nature Conservation in Nepal. Through its network of field offices throughout Annapurnas area, it had remained a pride of people even after 1990 democratic Upsurge. However, the Maoists claim that the Royal family has been getting millions worth of royalties during the Panchayat era and continue to hold its control. The experts considered ACAP a textbook example in Nature conservation.

The Maoists attacked the ACAP offices in Bhujung (May 2002) and set fire to a tourist resort of the Pokhara valley. Coupled with this arose the problem of fake Maoists who saved extorted money from tourists in the name of Maoists. The confusion multiplied.

Interestingly my fresh book of poetry, *The Lake Fewa and a Horse*, might appear very nostalgic and quixotic to the readers who have never actually seen this dream world. Even a manuscript of my *Annapurna Poems* that I'm preparing has started looking distant, otherworldly— an archival item.

Tied with these artistic complexities are the physical issues. Annapurnas has kept me physically fit, agile like a bird. It has breathed its fresh silence into the mouth of my poetry. Annapurnas is a celebration of a silence that connects our breaths to the soul of the gods. However, I am afraid over two years the flame of my breath has started wavering...

* * *

Spring 2008

Walking in the Pokhara Bazaar or sauntering by the Lakeside appears an epilogue to the countless journeys I have made in the Annapurnas sanctuary.

Unfortunately, or maybe fortunately, I've forgotten my digital camera back in Kathmandu. To mock at my inability, the massive ranges of snow-laden Annapurnas emerge in a spotlessly clean air and continue to gaze at me all day long. A colossal mass of a cosmic figure looms over the Valley.

Almost envious of the Pokhara people, I walk in a reverie. The still moment of the ever-wavering mountain ranges gawking at me stretches into a glorious day. The face of the mountain breaks into irresolute tapestry of sunlight and rain, shadow and shape. The clouds making and breaking the face of the giant goddess, whose glaciers feed our world, replenishing the granary stores of the Subcontinent.

Yet there were times when I was afraid to go into the Sanctuary, first about two decades ago because I feared the rigorous mountain life and later more recently because it had become the stronghold of the Maoist insurgency.

Unfortunately, the moment I decided to give the final touches to my Annapurna Poems in 2004, the things were not as bright. Gandrung village had turned into a ghost town, and the Gorepani and the rest of the region quaked ominously from the operations of the insurgent and the Military. I did meet some of the insurgents. They appeared ordinary looking people, bent to charm any new comer in the region with their party songs and exhort additional entry fee from the tourists holding the ACAP permits.

The local people seemed strangely quiet and only sheepishly complained of the food and accommodation that they had to dole out to the insurgents. Even today, after the Jana Andolan and the Peace dialogues and the Democratic rhetoric, the cadres continue to seek donations from the people in the Annapurna region. The hoteliers and lodge owner seem more vocal and critical of the cadres' attempt to exhort money, food, and accommodation.

Walking by the Lakeside or threading through the forest leading to the spacious Buddhist Stupa that keeps counting the myriad moods of the blue-eyed Fewa below, I look out at the almost supernatural stretch of the snow, vegetation, and water.

Where would I find a world as beautiful as this? Where else would the goddess find a refuge if not here? Where else in the world would I make my little Annapurna poems from the fiber of my bones and breath of my helpless words?

Wordless, I walk the courtyard of the hilltop stupa where a plump tourist lies lazily on a soft carpet of grass. In each fold of the Annanpura range, I recognize the place, the people struggling for bare survival in each crevice. In each crack a poem that I wrote or a narrative that I wove to make a sense of the eternally spiritual life of the sanctuary.

My head bows in reverence to the spirit of snow that gave me enough food to eat, to fill my mind, a mission to survive for the rest of my life.

Kathmandu, 2008

—**Yuyutsu RD Sharma**
www.yuyutsu.de
yuyutsurd@yahoo.com

Acknowledgements

The idea of publishing *Annapurna Poems* was always on my mind. However, the idea took a concrete shape 2004 when my mentor, distinguished American poet David Ray asked me to apply for the Rockefeller Fellowship.

The moment I mentioned Annapurna Poems as the proposed project, he leapt up with joy and thought it to be a wonderful book in the making. Hence, first and foremost, I am thankful to David Ray and The Rockefeller Foundation for inspiration and support to publish the book in its current shape. Poet Judy Ray also deserves a special mention for her constant support and inspiration.

The idea of publishing poems on a specific Himalayan range isn't very popular one in my parts of the world. In fact, when I stared visiting the region and wrote first few poems on the harsh trails, people thought either I was out of my mind or obsessed with something other than the mountains in the region.

Even the people there couldn't believe I was visiting the area for purly creative purposes. They guessed either I was visiting a relative or was on a pilgrimage to the sacred Muktinath shrine. Some others took me to be a Development officer from a Kathmandu-based INGO.

Still some less sympathetic ones guessed I had some female Yeti or a mountain Muse hidden in some hidden canyon. Otherwise why would one undertake such arduous treks in the Himalayas?

Most of the local people take mountain trekking to be bad karma from the past life, a hardship that one must try to overcome. No wonder a few educated professionals ever opt to be stationed in any of these remote districts. Kathmandu remains the ultimate destination for the majority of the Nepalese population and people from the remote regions are often looked at with distrust or disbelief.

But the Annapurnas came like a blessing in my life. With the Rockefeller Foundation fellowship not only could I travel in Europe, I also found my German Photographer and friend Andreas Stimm for my mountain poetry with whom I have published a trilogy of coffee-table books on the Himalayas. I am indebted to Andreas Stimm for giving me my first European Publisher on a grand style. I am also grateful to Epsilonmedia for generous support to pursue my mountain frenzy.

Gratitude is also expressed to His Excellency Mr. Keith Bloomfield, the then British Ambassador to Nepal and Her Excellency Mrs. Genevieve Charbonneau Bloomfield and Mr. David Ward, Charge de Affairs, the British Embassy at the time for kindly launching two of my books on the region in spite of all the hardships that country faced at that time. I am also thankful to Irish Ambassador His Excellency Kieran Dowling for timely support and generosity.

Scores of people helped me promote the books on the Annapurna region in Europe and America and I am grateful to them for fueling the fires of my imagination. I am especially indebted to Susan Garfield, Pilar Palacia, Cathal O Searcaigh, Carol Rumens, Pascale Petit, Fiona Sampson, Clyde Rose, Maggie Hindley, Eddie Woods, Hans Plomp, Robin and Elizabeth Carlin-Metz, Harry Zevenbergen, Evald Flisar, Christopher Emmrich, John Clarke, Rex Brown, Axia, Monica Heynderickx, Kees van der Fleece, George Spruce, Mark Leslie, Seymour Mayne, Jennifer Langer, Ronny Someck, Nilli Cohen, Amma Thekla Eick, Leonard Trawick, Suzanne DeGaetano, Jack Harte Dáithí Ó hÓgáin, Cathal McCabb Micheal O'Siadhail, Einar Moos, Martine Laurent, Jim Haynes, Fred Johnston, Gaye Facer, Bruce Bayley, Kathy Smith, Judith Mok, Randall Maggs, Agnes Meadows, Nicole Barrière, Dr. Nickel Eckhart, John Paul, Kadija George, Dimen Shine, Kees van der Vlies, Ursula McSweeney, Caroline Vogal, Merik van der Torren, Sarah Dobbs, Jordan Zinovich, Olga Paterson, Richard Livermore, Veronica Aranda, Patricia Foster, Sandy Serafini, Inara Cedrins, Alistair Spencer, and Annica Johannesson.

Thanks are also due to Nirmal Kanti Bhattacharje, Dr. Tara Niraula, Binny Kurian, AJ Thomas, Rohit Gurung, Harry Adhikary, Shiva Dhakal, Adona M, Hom Paribag, Abha Eli, Sharad Pradhan, Manoj Dahal, Raj Kumar Baniya, Padma Gautam, Bharat Neupane, Lekhnath Bhandari, Shyam Rimal and Prakesh Sindhuliya for creative support.

Special thanks to Pradeep K Bhandari and Nani Maiya Bhandari, Raju and Shova, Kumar and Chetna Bahandari, Shreejana and Shakti, Yugank and Sukrity for making my life work.

Kathmandu, 2008   - **Yuyutsu RD Sharma**

Contents

for
Yugank & Sukrity

Annapurna Poems

PART ONE
Little Paradise Lodge

In the Mountains

1.

Fragile my eyeglasses
fragile and foreign
I take them off;
There's a speck of a scar in them.

On the mule path
I take them off
to face the green
stretch of mountains
beneath the saddle of Annapurnas.

From the balcony
of clay plastered hut I see
a Sun rise in the clear sky of my life.
This is where last spring
a rainbow appeared
and seconds later
a Sun set at the same spot.
A huge Sun-sized moon
crept from behind the mountain
and lingered like a cherry-faced child
peering over the courtyard of Annapurnas,
this gorge of the River Modi.

Fragile my eyeballs;
fragile and tainted with the speck
of a bleeding tear
from my mother who left me lately.

I close my lids
and see her face in the courtyard.

2.

Five colored Buddhist flag
flutters in the moonlight.
In the adjoining room
you make love to your husband.
I recall the day
I had seen you naked
in the courtyard, naked
to your plump waist, sitting
like a goddess of granary
massaging your plump body,
glistening peaches of your breasts.

Little child lay close,
basking in the Sun.

3.

Out from the balcony
I see fragment of a cloud
stuck like a poet
in the green crotch
of the gorge, utterly alone.

Bridge

Rickety bridge
a lonely heir to my secret world.

Rickety bridge
an abandoned leaf in forest of my gloom

quaking like
shoulders of a hillside porter

thrumming like
strings of a blind singer

waking from sleep
in the slums of screaming cities…

Exasperated, I approach
wet spongy openings of your breezy body

moistened mouth
of a water spout oozing energy

On the rim of a valley's
bellybutton, a hot spring

odor
of earth's secret sex

waft of fragrance
stemming from a forest

buried
beneath centuries of snow

Rickety bridge
lonely heir to my secret sanctuaries

palaces of pleasure
in the hidden valleys,

rainforests and plateau beyond

a threadbare foreword to
my fleshy book of living and dying.

Snow

Snow from Annapurnas's
saddle melted in our kisses.
A blue magpie flashed past our vision,
in its wings drops of joy
from our new found world.
Sunflowers lifted their heads up
to make out meaning of our mirth
in the dark Shangri-La balcony.
The news of our love spread
in the valley of gods like
song of the laughing thrush,
chattering magpie's trick.
The snow peaks we imagined
from the sanctuary of our naked bodies
Little Paradise Lodge atop Kimrong Khola
hot springs down below
in the crotch of the green glades —
all hidden beneath blanket of Monsoons.
Our minds mingled, our mouths met
our eyes shared a sight of what
the Rains had veiled from our sight.
I cupped your tiny hillocks
in the dark, waited through the silence
of long hillside night to see our prayers
answered in the dawn
clear view of snow peaks aflame
from the sheen of your white breasts.

Little Paradise Lodge

My pen frozen against
the daggers of Annapurnas...

On an oblong shapeless plank chopped
from a sandal wood tree trunk and used as a table

I place my elbows
and hold my face in my hands.

Blinding snows of the Annapurna Ridge,
Hyunchali, shining in the eye of my mind,

I sit in the spacious courtyard of your paradise lodge,
deciphering the shrill notes of birds in the mossy trees.

One bird initiates a lilting note
like our meeting while
other lets loose a racket of breath-whistles
ending with question tags—
Can I stay longer, at least one more day,
in your little paradise lodge?

Two birds playing in the crimson cherry tree
stir a chord that seems
like opening up of the blossoms
of our bodies—Would you take me away and marry me?

But what about the electric whistle,
this cicada's constant chirr,
the struggle of our breathless bodies

against dark soot of the night?
The pigeons strutting freely in your courtyard
coo like exhausted porters
climbing the mule paths in the singing gorges.
Their guttural quataquatantankua—
they seem to be using human language,
a kind of hushed speech that robbers might use.

Love, in the courtyard of your little paradise lodge
I see the silence turning flowers into daggers

A herd of cows shuffles past me in a joyous mood
festive like young girls going to a hillside fair
saying — Don't go away, Dai,
we would be back until dusk with presents…

A cuckoo passes overhead – its distinct ka-ka-ka –
Please do not leave me alone.
I am utterly alone,
stuck on the last mountain of the world

And beyond me just one more mountain
where they say a deity lives
guarding a tiny turquoise lake.
And thereafter nothing but
realm of melting snows
where the souls of the gods live.

Lost Lovers

Your face
wears airs of a blossom

elegance
of a dandelion

majesty
of a sunflower

drowse
of a blue mimosa

your eyes
have stolen fires from the Himalayan lightning

your body
has kissed moistened lips of clear creaks

Your face seems familiar, love,
as you sit opposite me on a roadside teashop…

Your face,
how could I forget your face?

Slowly I recall how
it looked in the rush hours of my youth,

how you smiled
or rolled your eyes in awe

Years ago did I make
a promise and never returned

Those promises I made
as we sat beneath the forest of rhododendrons,

my life
aflame from the hearth of your body

glowing from the rush
of fresh blood in my heart.

Today as you pull your blouse
and give your long white breast to your child

I recall
the mark I left there,

a bruise resembling a memory
or a promise of homecoming.

Over the decade your face
has grown ample and wise like a shaman's drum

while barefoot I scampered
on the famished roads of many a mad metropolis.

You look a beauty
even today, resembling the ageless magnificence of snow.

Blood shamefully
rushes to your face

as you too get close to
a passing thought that turns into a revelation

Or love, is it the basket
full of wet firewood that you lift

on your back
before picking up the baby crawling on the trail…

Did we, dear one, separate like fires from a flame
to meet like bleeding mules on the trails of hardship
                                                    and hunger…

Her Guest's Greed

Beneath the glare
of the eternal snow

in a roadside restaurant
along teahouse trails

a plump squint-eyed
Sahuni squats on a straw mat

a tribal goddess
of granary, dressed

exposing fragments
of her hidden Paradise —

snowy shins, cleavage
of her floral fields

eating her Dalbhat meal
from a brass plate

and not-so-deep
bowl of red chili-sauce

frugal substitute
for chicken /vegetable soup.

Flower-faced woman
supple as Aphrodite, or Urvashi,

Goddess of enduring fish eyes,
she scoops steaming rice in her hand

dips it in a bowl of
lentil soup, takes a kiss

of red chili-sauce
and hurls a ball of rice

into her mouth
with a jerk.

An old colorless rooster
scrawny, faceless, featherless,

stands nearby
on his limp leg, like

a Sufi saint meditating, nearly
shaking his gloom onto her plate...

Deviously, he hovers
over her plate, unable to hold

horses of his hunger,
unable to let her finish

and leave a grain
or two in the plate...

Enticed by the scene,
a passerby stops, asking

the price of mineral water bottle,
distracting her attention,

ordering a Pepsi…

In a flash, the rooster twists
his ugly neck, in an electric swoop

steals a peck at her plate
and instant after, cool and cosmic,

resumes his Sufi position…

She merely brushes her hand
as reflex, shoots an abuse

as if he were an urchin,
or an unruly family member

and resumes eating.

The rooster once again waiting
on his limp leg, her nose running,

her cleavage sweating
from midday heat and hot chili sauce

and from the thirst of her new guest ,
an added character to the scene,

hovering over
the vessel of her body, waiting…

Running ahead of the Roads racing...

An ambulance
carrying the dead crosses my path

at Dumre, Nayapul, Beni...

That's the first omen
of the tarred road that

races like a snake
of fire into the groin of Annapurnas...

Pungent, piercing
like my guilts, stench of mule dung

and urine hits my nostrils,
fertilizing the flowers of my faith

along the dusty mule paths of my life...

Fat bumblebee buzzes
on the edge of an insane ecstasy.

Riverside Lodge closed,
Insurgents cook their gruel there

in the cabin that once
sheltered galaxies of my joy.

Like the life-lines,
the distances shortened

Roads widened,
stone steps flattened

Riverbeds rolled
into dusty fields

Did they bring equipments
to wipe out carpets of butterflies

sanctuaries of fat cockerels
and chattiest grandmas of the region

Waterfall beds that
smelled of the birth of fresh fish

empire of moss, moisture and mash?

Rickety expansion bridge
squeaks as they flung bulldozers

across the pathways
of angels and tribal horse hooves,

choking lifelines
of laughing thrush and other singers of Paradise.

One last time I smile,
One last time I borrow

a pinch
of salt from a roadside shop

expecting
a bite of long leeches along the famished roads.

Birethanti

In the mud-plastered room
by the roaring river I opened my anguished eyes.

Outside seven
colored Buddhist flag fluttered.

The river tireless, thundering
without a trace of grief.

Hillside roosters
punctual, announcing the dawn.

Possessing floral
faces of riverside birds

local women up
from their warm beds, cooking.

I too got up
and through a mossy hill path

in the backyard
reached the deafening edge of the river

and watching
the spray of the white surf

on greasy crotches
of huge mossy rocks

started singing
a song from a cheap Hindi movie,

whose notes soon splintered

into a shaggy cry
that I cried and cried,

coughing out
the cacophony of cruel cities

until from my lungs
without my knowing started coming

thundering music of
a solemn rage of the roaring river.

Christ's Cross

Two sacks
of rice

crossed
on a fragile-boned

Grandma's back
moving ahead

like an big wounded
beetle on the feverish slope

of Ulleri's
steepest climb.

Mule Range

Burden
of nightshift's filth

reckless treks
in the vortex of weight whorls

endless agony
of drifting in the kingdoms of snow

bare bargain
of blue dawns and emerald ranges

for bleeding eyes
of dark tunnels

of spinach plies pots
of curd jerkins of fresh milk

for beds
of liquor- vomits

and a lifetime
of illness in a village

on a hilltop
drooling in a drowse

that's death.

PART TWO

Glacier

Advent

Poetry died before you did.
It had probably foreseen yours.
Unease grabs my throat,
I can't breathe; morsel
of agony stuck in it.

Your jaws unhinged, your twisted
mouth shaking to hold
even a spoonful of glucose.

First Page

First page I take out
after your exit, in tears.

First page,
agony fresh
but page blank.

I can't simply
lift this pen of mine up.

Flash of your wounded eyes—
clips of my finger tips
exerting to hold the wrinkled flaps
of your eyelids, inside out,
unleashing a rain of blood
spluttering blank spaces of my wailing sky.

A Morning Walk

Leaving behind
the bed of white lotus

and wheezing
partner of my sleep

I rushed out
towards the bridge

freshly built over
a golden stream.

But on finding
a funeral pyre

burning on its
emerald edge

I closed my eyes
and like some Buddha

in the dark interior
raised my shaking,

invisible hands
to salute

the great master
Death.

Fish

Plump goldfish
gather in a blue pond,

greed
of a city's mangled commune.

A silence stretches
its muscle, wetting
bones of a bleeding spring.

Allergic, sun-scarred,
they keep fattening
on the fungus
of a forest of inertia.

Here in the mountains
by the river's bemused edge
I remember a promise
I made to my mother years ago.
She died in the fierce eye
of an rancorous summer
counting stars
in the blistering sky of my youth.

Wives wait the final winter
of my rot, opening up
the greed
of their slithering fish.

I return to a poem
I postponed decades ago
to touch the mating serpents
slithering on the tip of illicit door
called death.

River: Morning

Cruel river
knows each time

I come to brood
over her roaring waters

each time I come
to her deafening banks

to gleam my dreams
over the plump flanks of her warm body

each time I come
to pour last of my life's salt

in the ringing gorges
of her sonorous frame,

a bone breaks
in my smoldering chest

and a wrinkle appears
across the shriveled leaf of my life.

River at Night

Dark night
I cannot see the river.

I can only
hear it thundering rumble.

A water well explodes
enamored in the fleshy

clutch of fluffy
clouds, making a cave of this gorge.

Only fingers of the fireflies
illuminate its shape, the wild limbs,

as the river fumbles
curled around the hefty thighs of the night

to find a wink of sleep.

Harlot

In the dark of the night
on a sullen turn of a slope

I speed my steps up
and leave her behind

"Impotent!" she yells.

A dagger of sunlight
singes ocean of my ageing eyes.

In my brain start
reeking a million defunct moons.

A humid smell
of a menstruating fish comes

from the earth just wet
from the first showers of the Monsoons.

Rains

This summer I missed
advent of the rains

rumble of a flooded river Modi
tumbling boulders upside down in its anguished bed

clap of lightning lashing
perfumed lions of the canyons

rush of the fresh skin
over the denuded chest of the hills

canopy of snow in the Annapurnas
rustling to make a soft song of moonlight..

This summer they held me up
in the deserts of their skyscrapers.

I stood in the sweltering alleys
of Connaught Place

recollecting poems
of a forgotten ecstasy,

my face in the dark
feeling tips of snow sacred fishtails of Machapuchchare.

A poem of fireflies
or an ugly pageant

of powerful crows
from the illicit Academy of national lies?

A wine shop of verses
or corridors of an illegitimate polity

turning fire-spitting
lions into Coca Cola tin cans?

Rain Raven Razors.

Rain Rivers Ridges.
Rain Run Run

I cried and woke up
to the smell of cow dung

odor of porters sweating
in bazaars of the walled city

building a Babylon for soft nailed
vultures of crumbling economies.

In the Ghalib's streets
I shared his songs with the wandering vendors

carrying pitchers
and wounded water-wells from the parched villages.

Bejeweled witches of Indraprastha
or a little house on a hilltop where

my young moons keep
bouncing over the rainbow of her eyelashes?

I extend my secret bottle of wine
to the barefaced flutter of a saffron flag

and with the moonfaced madmen from the Red Fort
all through the sweltering nights

roam the streets of the cursed city
measuring hidden Yamuna of its bleeding guilt.

Range and Romance of Rains

Yes, it's true.
Today I do not want to write.
I've waited the day all year long.
I've waited for the rains
on the simmering threshold of the summer.
I stop on the mule paths
as I go past the slender waterfall.
I hear the gurgle, noise of a building crashing,
of a mountain changing its side in sleep.
The sky turns into a watery cave roof.
I wait for its arrival on the flagstone steps.
I stand like a maniac,
like a Sufi saint shedding bucketfuls of tears.
I look at the sky,
the whole of the Western horizon
a vast sheet of black clouds loaded with water.
A giant wave of a turbulent ocean
that climbed up the steep hills.
I wait for the waters to crash
my gigantic lusts for the waters.
I dance like a firefly. I dance like Meera,
like Confucius, like Ryokan, and like Rimal.
Like a young woman who has just found her true love.
Rain. Rain. Rain. Rain. Rain.
I weep for the thirsty crow that died this morning.
I laugh at the jackals howling in the corridors of Authority.
I leer at my enemies sulking at their tables of deceits.
I holler at my followers, the ones who have kept me alive.

I dance to the moves of my defeat.
I forgive the ones with their daggers drawn.
And I dance like a devil in rage, in the rain.
I dance in tune to the range and romance of the rains,
Mad, alone in the singing gorges of Annapurnas.

An Old Lover/an Older Dream

Your hour with me was a proverbial eternity.
Words, wounded, charred, mangled
like hubris of a vanquished sky.
A feel of limbs getting infirm
like bones of a century-old oak tree
spooled by hi-tech city's harrowing upbringing.
More than a decade ago
on the edge of a river I had sucked those lips
and learnt fresh language of a river's century.
I had cupped your breasts
white and goose-like, fresh shimmer of *Kailash* snow.
You were in a hurry
to rush to Hawaii on a scholarship.
I stayed back to count wounds of my people
dancing in crooked *mandala* of hunger.
Years rolled down the terraced oat fields
like human heads chopped from dispossessed torsos.
I stayed back to recall the names
of the roads that had once been rivers.
I stayed behind to get infected from a breeze
that once ululated throbs of tired tribal.
You say you are married to a German now.
My teeth grow weak in my mouth.
Or is it the infirmity in my feeble bones,
my inability to pick up
a ten-year-old daughter of mine?
You say you are married now.
I scribble my anonymity
on the graffiti of your body.
A dry leaf flashes in my eye, shakes

a string of tears and drops dead at the feet,
like an intense decade, anguished and ashamed.

I shall not write a poem...

Ulysses lies
on the glistening shelf, waiting to be read.

A speck of trivia
shoots eye of the cosmic sleep of a nebula.

I shall not write
a line of poetry...

Page lies blank, blighted
by mediocrity of cynical clerk-critics.

Page shrunken
from idiocy of a defunct democracy.

Page that would demand expansion,
scrutiny of a lifetime's fiction.

Brain conceives magnanimous plots
but page refuses to listen.

Page of a naked life,
a poets' eccentric, unforgivable audacities.

Page that would smash
frivolous forts built by a university of frogs.

Page that waited
for a dawn to at last acknowledge

a moment of truth
hooting through endless curfews

clamped on his outrageous life.

Page lies wet today
naked in the rain on a thundering night

on a mulepath in remote Chitra where
local wine shops vomit lies, history's ugly bile.

I shall never ever
write a line in this country.

Rain Poem in My Room

Writing a rain poem
amidst brooks and flowers

dancing in my little room
isn't entirely impossible.

Sloshing fall
of my five-year-old son's laughter

on the slanting pen
of my long hand

and his tussles and
scuffles with his tingling sister

crackle like a clap
of lightning on the table of my imagination.

Writing a spring poem
of Monsoon showers

in my little room
couldn't be impossible.

Writing a splatter
of raindrops on the green grass

as my son sits
in the window and looks out,

pouring torrent of syllables
and writes the watercourses of words

C-i-c-a-d-a, C-h-o-r-u-s,
F-r-o-g, F-u-n-g-u-s, F-i-r-e-f-l-y

in blank sheets of
life's notebooks seems altogether possible.

Writing songs
of Monsoons in my own courtyard

where my eleven-year-old daughter
imagines months of her forthcoming youth,

swings of success
on the ledge of life's bridge isn't impossible.

Imagining fleecy
clouds of spring

in the green glades
of her body should not be impossible

She changes every minute
like a monsoon sky, like grass

or pine trees on the hills
of her adolescence, shooting upwards

like brush of pine tree tops
bursting through the clouds

to kiss iridescence of a sky
that shall one day

become her world,
our world, her sky where golden birds

of her life's perennial spring
shall sing, sharing sweet bread of her dreams.

A Lonely Brook

A lonely brook flows
towards a desolate night...

On its bank
sits a woman with a shop open,

doorless, naked,
painting her face in this wilderness,

trying to wash
the drunken breath of her husband,

knowing in the stony
square up in the village

a cock crushes
a proud hen under his awesome sway...

By the edge of
a lonely brook

a lonely woman
waits for a stranger to come

and burst
the ice frozen between her thighs

to make a flame
of her cold sleep

to suck the fog
of her lungs with the fire of his tongue...

On the edge
of a lonely brook at dusk

with a shop open
doorless, naked

sits a young woman
lighting a lamp to illuminate

the dark hill paths
from where a snow leopard shall come

pouncing through
the greasy bushes and fragrant ferns

to put the plump
forest of her shimmering body aflame...

A lonely brook flows
towards a desolate night..

My Mataji's Last Smile

The sky stranded with rain-soaked clouds,
Ma, puffs of your tangled grey hair.
Water they carry over the rim
of this frightened valley are tears undyingly
held in the sockets of my eyes.
My last kiss on the crisscross
of your wrinkled cheeks as you lay on the funeral pyre
is all I remember. "Oye, don't you place
such heavy logs on my Mataji's tender chest."
They made me put your body aflame,
and hit your skull with a pointed log.
They said it's forgetting, these rituals
of touching horizons and coming back
to our earthly thresholds. Rituals!
Rituals! and cruelty, oh cruelty!
Next morning your ashes flew
over charred fields of a summer countryside
and struck the pulp of my eyes.
Now yellow wasps flitting in the empty courtyard
drink from your open, dust-coated water trough.
In your absence I noticed
a toad enter our house, like an agent of doom,
Hunting cockroaches, an army of them,
skittering beneath your extinguished stove.
At hospital a million Suns shone
as you gasped for your last breath.
My spoonful of glucose lies, stale as an anthill.
Are you still around, Ma, like those spirits
roving around your beloved son all the time?
The dog stirs abruptly as I open the gate

of the tiny garden before my house, alarmed.
At night thunder races over the reaches
of the valley's torpid sky, frightening
my innocent kids playing 'antakshari'.
Snails keep a hushed watch at my doorsteps.
Caterpillars climb up the windows
of the house. And it keeps raining
relentlessly, like my tears uninterruptedly.
Would they never explode to make
butterflies of my secret guilt's grief?
For days I lay prostrate on the spot you left me,
on the cold floor of our ancestral Baithak.
The milk you hung over the line
to make your morning tea has curdled.
Good morning! Mataji, Good Morning!
My lovely lovely Mataji!
Did you sleep well last night?
Next morning I open the gate of my house
to inspect devastation wrought by last night's
lightning that lashed the tulips of my garden.
Iron gate creaks as I move out
and find an oriole dead at my feet,
wearing innocence of your last smile.

Ghandrung: Water-Play

"A little home in the Himalayan hills"
reads the register in Shangri-la Lodge

The threshold breathes
fragrant through breezy load of flowers.

An old grandma's smiling eyes
accept you with a shake of her dangling nosering.

In the meandering lanes
of this village a dusty boy turns up abruptly

and raises his hands, *Namaste*!
forgetting his nose running since Second World War.

Docile rooster clutched
under her armpit

the young girl
of the scarlet shawl waits

for the colorful procession
of mules carrying cartons of Tuberg beer to pass.

In the spacious courtyards
of this village I hear shy singing streams.

A furious wind comes raging
from the saddle of Annapurnas

and mingles with the water-play
of little streams in these-courtyards,

a toned hushed opera of war cries
of valiant heroes killed in distant wars,

frozen fury of blood melted
and gone cold to make a little soft song of life.

Ghorepani

Is it incessant rain
or a mourning monsoon brook ?

Is it a Yeti following
your trail in the desolate mountains

or a crisp leaf
rolling on the breath of icy winds ?

Is it a mat rolled up
by a sheet of drying millet

or a newly born baby
asleep after an oily massage ?

Is it a huge cucumber
left to dry on the rooftop by a busy housewife

or a fat rooster
dozing by a brown cat in the warm sunlight ?

Is it blaze of
of a khukuri in the emerald green glade

or fragrant
flash of her shimmering nose ring ?

Is it a dragonfly
skittering through

the golden stalks
of ripe paddy fields

or a shivering sickle
reaping misfortune of famished fields ?

Are these crooked
limbs of a burly bear

or mossy boughs
of a juniper in the forest of Rain ?

Is it an iridescent
feather shed by some blue jay

or a wandering
shaman's cruel craft ?

Is it cackle
of a lonely thrush

or my own breath
weaving a song of silence ?

Desolate Mountains of Mustang

This poem I write
for the porters of the popular trail

holding the rusting bars
of a squeaking wooden bridge

never ending song
of Modi Khola roaring in me,

a waterfall
with the crystal cry

of a new born baby
falling from unimaginable heights

on the simmering lump
of lead, my heart.

A bird hooting flies
through my brain as if having known a secret.

I tear through the film
of butterflies on the mule path of Kaligandaki

and climb the fragrant mountains to find
the Sun, a plump plaything,

crawling like a baby
around the glaciers of Annapurna.

I walk along the river,
chilly winds slapping my eyelashes,

when suddenly a fan fire
of visions sparkles in my brain

and I climb the mountains,
step by step, breathless,

my kidney beating
like tiny cymbals to bargain

frugal grains
for a sack full of potatoes

I carry on my back...

But what's it that I hear?

A jingle of the bells of a stupa,
a chorus of cherry-faced hill women,

a wedding party
in the wilderness of this frozen desert ?

Or a prayer procession
of Lamas of Jomsom ?

Aye, no, a horde of mules
and donkeys, yak tails furling over their heads,

speeding towards me
like some furious demon

to hit me off the track
and burst me into pieces like a fragile vase,

in the pit
of the green vale ....

And thus I become
an angry wound of the hills

cursed to wander
like orphaned winds through

frozen passes
and desolate mountains of Mustang.

Father

My hair go aflame
as he hiccups and breathes the last of this earth.

A gray wart appears on my forehead.

I clasp your cold palms
to feel blackout of your blood vessels.

On your chest I burst
a silent pitcher of my life's sleep

Darkness,
a savage silence of *Sunya's* eternal ocean.

I glisten your rubbery body
from honey, curd and milk of seven rivers;

a tear keeps rolling endlessly
on the naked wound of my secret grief.

For the last time I hold
this face of yours in my trembling hands;

blast of a wail
ravages sunlight of my faith.

On your body I place
heavy logs damp from a history of vanquished hearts.

In the crack of your still mouth
I drop grain of a rainbow

and light the last fire
that shall blacken quiet pages of my youth.

I hit the center of your skull
aflame in the spluttering pyre

to ignite a bejeweled passage to eternity.

On the flooded banks of the Ganges
I knead your limbs all over again;

I make your head
heart, hands, life-veins, lines of your fate.

From the mantras of my breaths
I feed hunger of your blood vessels

and see you go alone
along the blazing fields of *The Garuda Purana*

eating crumbs of the blessed food
lost in the memories of my childhood

when once you has lifted me
up in the fragrant stretch of the blue hillside air

and probably for the first time
in your life, smiled…

Mules

On the great Tibetan
salt route they meet me again

old forsaken friends ...

On their faces
fatigue of a drunken sleep

their lives worn out,
their legs twisted, shaking

from carrying
illustrious flags of bleeding ascents.

Age long bells clinging
to them like festering wounds

beating notes
of a slavery modernism brings:

cartons of Iceberg, mineral water bottles,
solar heaters, Chinese tiles, tin cans, carom boards

sacks of rice
and iodized salt from the plains of Nepal Terai.

Butterflies of
the terraced fields know their names.

Singing brooks tempests
of their breathless climbs.

Traffic alert
and time-tested, they climb

carrying
dreams of posh peacocks

pamphlets
of a secret religious war

filth
of an ecologist's sterile semen

entire kitchen
for a cocktail party at the base camp

defunct development
agenda of guilty donors

the West's weird visions
lusting for an instant purge.

Stone steps
of the mountains embossed

on their drugged brains,
like lines of aborted love

scratched
on the historic rocks of waterspouts.

Starry skies
of the dozing valleys know

the ache
of their secret sweat.

Sunny days
along the crystal rivers
taste
of their bleeding eyes.

Greatest fiction
of the struggling lives lost,

like real mules
clattering their hooves on the flagstones,

in circling
the cruel grandeur

of blood thirsty
mule paths around the glacial of Annapurnas.

Modi Khola

River millenniums
have feared, a shaman's charm.

River they conquered,
flash of the sweaty limbs,

glaze
of a cutting utensil's edge.

River they worshipped before
flinging over its roaring frame

a squeaking
suspension bridge.

River that created
turquoise looking glasses for them

to comb every morning
the enigmas of their dark lives.

River agreed to spill over
in their breaths, in their songs,

in the torrents
of their struggling blood.

River spread out
to solve the sums of their children, tendrils of turmoil.

River forecast
omens for them, death, birth, move, remove.

River made
calendars, festivals, magic, mandalas for them.

River that counted time
for them, years, lives, longings.

River that brought them
birds, clouds, fireflies, silence.

River that possessed
in its rumble uranium of rain-soaked thunderclaps.

River whose permanent
paramours were those lush green mountains;

charred and shaved today
mourning over the river that shall die now

strangled by the dusty road
coming like a noose around its neck

a lethal fang of dam-dragons
hissing to put the saga

of green canopies
of rainforests aflame.

River

Between your marble
shoulders and my hairy chest

the river roaring,
tears, tears, tears...

Between your mellowing
mouth and my scented tongue

a night of flames
and flesh, flesh, flesh ...

Between your hefty thighs
and my throbbing hands

clouds drunk
from the forests of rhododendrons.

Between your almond eyes
and my warm mouth

rain dropping like pearls
on the plump leaves of the jungle.

Between your shimmering skin
and my dark hair grass greener

than the greenest parakeet
growing yellowish from incessant rain.

Between your nights by
the impotent pillow of your husband

and my crazed headpiece
a poem of spring that shall fill my deep wounds,

sprouting flowers, flowers, flowers ...

Between your tulips
and my fragrant pen

a brain-fever bird's
crazed cry, mad, mad, mad...

Between the sparkle
of your teeth and my sleep

a rain coming
like roar of a starving steam

in the starless
summer gloom of the night.

Between your melon breasts
and thirst of my soft lips

the rage of the river
battering its head against the magic mountains.

Between your decisions
and my flickering lamps

the river mad
you, you poet, you bastard, go away !

Glacier

A hope
that someday I shall sprout

like a tree
on the edge of a remote hillside.

A hope
someday a Queen-of-the-Night

shall bloom in my chest
and suck all the smoke

I have inhaled
in these malignant cities.

A hope that someday
a just born brook shall clean

and wash
bacteria of greed in me.

A hope that someday
a Buddha meditating in the niche of a cairn

by the heap of the city
garbage shall shake his limbs

and walk away towards a village of eternity
to take another birth

to save me
from the shame of becoming a glacier.

Poem of Tender Flesh

The little lawn by
the thundering brook has withered,

blight of trust
and longing, a night of secret lust...

Glare of sunlight
baring the chest of a young mountain

ruins the romance
of writing hillside poems

in a world where wealthy wives
abort their brightest babes every month...

Standing in the middle
of my life's squeaking bridge, facing

the brilliance
of your plump white body

I foresee a season
of sterility, of drowning...

The dusk falls upon
the bright frame of the raging river

stifling jubilant
songs of mating river-birds.

I stand here,
white surf of Modi raging under my feet

facing round
hills of your breasts,

here from where I left
a year ago forgetting the smoke of the city

and smile of skyscrapers
on this riverside, here round

the creamy curve
of your ripe and round breasts,

a mellowing kiss
of your mulberries

in a secret room
of a tin-roofed house

full of fireflies
and sweet smell of blood-drenched flowers

a trick of poetry
that might turn truth

a reunion that shall
surge a wave of secret blood,

an onrush
of creativity

that shall make a tiny
poem of tender flesh and vibrant bones.

PART THREE
Sister Everest

Sagarmatha

The turquoise lake
that longs to belong to the ocean
trapped to see
dazzling face of the Everest.

The climbers from the world over
come to see their haggard faces
in the clear light of her crystal eyes
before facing the forehead of the Sky.

Way to Everest

Way to Everest
passes through steep dreams
of glaciers, salt waters'
lucent revolt against rigid rocks,
centuries of Sleep
finally waking up
with the Sherpa load
of entire earth
to shape life
pulsating as
Chiringphuti's earrings,
supple as her malleable lips,
intricate as lines
of aborted fate in her cracked heels.

Kala Patthar

The face
of water crashing
on the black phallus
of the rock where first time
before the birth
of the bird of vacuum
the demon goddesses
mated with the gigantic ape,
turning God's
semen of humanity,
the Sea,
into a solid mass,
the earth's third pole.

First Mountains, Mother Mountains

Stench of the burning hair
in the stretch of boundless snow.

Whose blood drops
amble through Yeti's trail?

Forehead of the sky besmeared
with massacre of a million dreams

Who are these who dance frenzied swirl
around the shaman's drum on the glacier?

The squeaking chicken
in the baskets of the porters

final fear of death
in the cage of rattling bones.

On the top of the world
I stand facing the gorgeous glacier

with my late
mother's smiling face.

God's plough

A dry leaf
rolls on the breath
of the wind as I walk
by roaring river's soft edge
in the gorge
wrought by God's
colossal plough
where Dudkosi
hums notes of lament
away from
the domain of Sutras
and malevolent cities
that can corrode
meaning out from
the river's
ruthless rush
to join the ocean
of humanity's discontent.

Sherpa Woman

Toothless Sherpa mother
let me sleep

deepest sleep
of my life

in her warm
doorless barn

lighted by moonlight
filtering through

the fractures
of her wooden walls.

Wind and Mist

Wind would never win.
It's the mist that rules here

In the domain of Lord of the underworld
it seeps into the corners,

cracks and crevasses, into my shoes,
in the pores of my skin. Mist, the mild spirit

like Namche Bazaar's little girl who
won me over with her cool stare

as I went down the slope,
defeated at the Silence's sprawling edge.

Gauri Shankar

Disturbed by the cries
of the imperial pheasant
Shankar woke from his deep sleep
and looked across the valley of Rolwaling .

Surely the young woman
playing with a stag in the blue distance
was his lost sister-in law, his precious little Gauri,
goddess-like and gracious, the one who had left home
after a petty family feud three days' ago.

He passionately
moved towards the valley.

From this end Shankar began to climb
while Gauri on the other was descending

Yes, yes, she's the one, the sister-in-law
he had been looking for all these days.

At one point they met—
Why did you leave in my absence?
He was about to ask.

But since a sister-in-law should
never ever face the elder brother-in-law barefaced,
Gauri blushed and instantly flung her shawl
over her face and then and there both froze
and became rocks.

The shawl of snow that Gauri
flung over her head did never break.

And on top of Shankar's enormous
black head snow never came to fall.

Eyes of Andreas' Chorten

Very human, hungry,
feeble, almost,

water like, fish like,
a just born baby's tear like

a charcoal geometry
on the palpable face of an upright glacier

pure and crystalline
Christ like, before Paul's murky shadow fell,

bemused eyes
older than horoscope of Siddhartha,

larger than the ocean
a female Yeti would have shed

before she was grabbed
and butchered by the monks

defeated by
the daggers of compassion

yantras of Sunya,
throttled by Boddhisattvas
 brutally wounded,
weary eyes of a human

buried beneath
debris of spiritual flagstones

and snow sheets
of savage civilizations

a ruthless tear
in a body, a bullet full of blood,

a rough hewn
creature grabbed first

thing in the morning
like Ganesha's head

and crucified before
it could have said a word

about history of mystery,
hunger and humanity.

Orange Falls

By the raging waterfalls
against the pure white
sheet of surf
she peeled orange
skin of her body,
and offered me
her pulp and citreous,
this just-made-holy-nun
named Catherine from Tyangboche.

On the slippery stones
I laid my bare knees
and silently ate
slice after slice
of the blessed fruit.

Deafening roar of the falls
wouldn't let us utter
or imagine a word.

Summit

'Truth left behind,
in the fragrant villages and the world'
I said to myself
after I climbed
the summit, weary and breathless,
wind whipping my eyes,
head giddy
from the inconceivable heights.
I bowed in awe
and positioned a primrose
on my Maya's
snowy chest. She smiled
at the folly of it all —
empty looks, childish arrogance
the blank stretch of
endless snow spaces,
and nothing beyond.
'Truth left behind, on the trail
in the fragrant villages and the world.'
She smiled and sent
me scuttling down
her mountains
dashing through alpine deserts
past green glades and
fermented canyons'
black undergrowth
where real life's eternal springs flow.

The Buddhist flag flutters

The Buddhist flag flutters
to the call of the barking deer

to the flight of the golden eagle
circling above Tyangboche, in the galaxies

of untouched unborn avatars.
The saffron flag quivers

to the hum of Dolma's
broom sweeping stone steps strewn

with palm leaves
and *Lays* plastic packs.

The rainbow flag wavers in the winds
of Bigu, weight of wasted centuries on its spine,

shaman's hollowed skull full of travelers' blood,
magical Yak's history of flying skins.

The flag furls on the way to Namche,
amused to see the growing greed

of Yeti, the fresh global food
it feeds on every morning of the new millennium—

STD, Internet, Cafes, Cakes, camera
and digital color's click, click...

On the trail to Everest
where Dharma bums walked past eternal springs
with their wayward dog-souls
the flag thrums its blade to see
porters left out freezing out in the cold,
fees charged in euros for entry of moving cameras
in Nirvana's historic courtyards.
It laughs to see Lama
forget the mantras it parroted all his life
and watch Baywatch and Bond in One
sipping Amstel beer instead of chhyang
from his favorite Yak's back
while outside all night long dismal snow falls
obstinately melting centuries of salt load
placed on the exhausted zopkioks' bleeding backs.

Everest Failures

In the mud floored porch
of a misty little shack

by the raging brook's
soft edge, peeling

the skin
of maize off, aflush

amidst its fluffy pile
sits a hillside mother

with a baby son
wailing in her lap.

She has
nothing but a kiss,

a soily
sloppy stinking kiss

to shut
this wailing kitten up.

Eernal Snow: Epilogue

The glaze of the snowy summits
in dark ink of the earth's sleep.
Thousands walked past
the grandeur of this exquisite nightmare
and wandered off like the buffalo brother
who climbed into the mountains with his twin's coat
and strayed to get incarnated as yak
in the alpine wilderness.
Or in an attempt to map every inch of her breast
without a warm quilt of solace or secret mantra
froze to eternity in God's colossal grave.
In naming, renaming or de-naming
the house of the Lord's soul, *Devatatama*,
they drew diagrams, sketched,
dreamt over the staggering heights,
raised questions—colonial, carnival,
existential and extra-territorial—'Because it's there'
They endorsed a cause, carried long knives, oxygen, eggs
tea, telephones, sirdars and frozen spaghetti.
Did they bleed in snow, lost limbs and lives
on the altar of *Chho-mo-lung-ma*,
Goddess of the winds of the world
for victory that wasn't theirs?
Did they bow down in humility
before her crotch, at Cho Oya,
Gorak Shep or Kala Pathar?
Did they remember their loved ones
in the last drowse of their dream's dairy—
Frances, Younghusband, Mallory,
Bullock, Bruce, Northen, Somervil, Irving, Hillary.
Was it their Karma journeys to the Gates of Paradise

like Pandvas from Mahabharata after winning a war
they lost to the vanquished?
Was God disguised as a dog as in Yudhister's case
and did they break a green twig before
setting foot on the Mother's torso?
And did they insist on the entry of the soul-dog
like illustrious Dharmraja to go for
the Elysium of eternal snow?.

Or just went up to "knock the bastard off."

PART FOUR
The Annapurna Man

Frankfurt

Freckled shell of God's city
turns out to be soft meat of a Donar.

I wipe myself clean
of the dust of miracles that I've carried
like a bird across the oceans.

"Having traveled so far
what difference you think there remains
between fiction and reality,
between shell and kernel?"
says George as his girlfriend blows
her cute nose unabashedly in my presence.

Sex shops, gay salons, Eros,
the nude sculptures in the balcony,
orgies in the underground metro stations,
the orgasms in the station toilet,
pointed tip of the blunt Turkish knife
on the soft throat of a newcomer.

In the square next to EU Commercial Centre
an artist draws his penny painting on the pavement
or a singer kicking his heels
at the top of his voice gets just a whistle
from a teenage girl, not sale of his CD.

Walking on the heels of hunger
he knows not it's an obsession here
to polish everything clean, including syllables

of survival he has picked up in this land
of chilled anger where once a man walked like a demigod
where once he dug graves for the living
where once he furled a fetid flag familiar
and fluttering unashamedly in my own land today.
In the chilled air I walk on the stony sidewalks
only to see my own shadow reflected
on the glassy walls of skyscrapers.
But Judith's soft voice touches the tail
of the horse where once a Buddha lived.
A touch of autumn
I've left behind in my own Annapurnas.
George sits home waiting for Susanna like a housewife.
Obediently he shops in the supermarkets, weighing
each penny like a grandma. He feeds the recycle machine
empty bottles to get a euro in return.
I start speaking a language of husbands
that I've mastered on the ghats of Ganges,
a secret invective, an uncanny repartee of bandits..
But Judith's face keeps flaring
like silvery peaks of Annapurnas,
fishtail of her golden head bobbing
like a halo of lust denied to humans.

De Zwarte Ruiter Cafe

They treated me like
a drunken lorry driver would

a nubile girl
from a remote Himalayan village.

"Can you call the dead,
you man from the Himalayas?" one of them hollered.

Raising her voice above the rocking music
in the cafe, other shouted, "Nonsense! Pure bullshit!"

"Look here, answer!" the former insisted,
"Can you stop my late Grandpa

from visiting my bedroom twice a month."

She held her friend's hand
to stop her from offering me a handshake

and raised her sleeveless plump arm
in the air as if holding a dagger

"Whooooo!" she cried, "I switch off the light
and whoooooo! There it comes— Whooooooo!

Can you tell me if the dead
can come back to disturb your peace?

Can you explain why I dream of crocodiles
with baby faces chasing me as I run miles and miles

of bleeding river's expanse ?
You man from the land of Yeti,"

she picked up her empty wine glass
and laying it beside an ashtray started naming objects:

"Okay, let's say this is my grandpa, the dead one,
but tell me, can he come back to visit me in my bedroom?

Do they exist,
these silent travellers of our disturbed sleep?"

Two young women of Den Haag kissed like lovers
and asked—"What does your Buddha say about this?"

They giggled and then a silence spread.

And I knew they wished me to wear
a shaman's feathered crown for my head

and dance round and round
for several centuries to avenge the atrocities

of the male Buddhas
in the corridors of history for them.

Space Cake, Amsterdam

"Don't panic," they said,
remain cool like your Krishna,
meditate maybe like Buddha,
uttering 'Om Mani Padme,' jewel in the lotus,
or lie down and relax
like Vishnu on the python-bed
to float on the ocean's currents,
buoyant on the invisible thread
of your breath in slow motion...

Millions of cats prowled around me.
Smoke from shared sex
and hashish joints stung my eyes.
Unsettling tongue
of an awkward fire fed my stomach.
I skidded queasily towards
towards the formidable edge,
unknown ominous frontiers of human life...

They laughed a secret laugh
behind my back – "Isn't it crazy that
this man from Kathmandu should get stoned
from a piece of space cake in Amsterdam?"

"Don't be serious, laugh,
celebrate the flame of life!" a woman's voice said.
"Hold my hand; I can imagine
you are alone on this trail.
I've been there once," she whispered.
Her tongue curled like a dry leaf in my ear

and crackled "How much did you take,
just a piece? I took thirty-eight grams once,
It can be crazy if you don't know it's coming.
Just don't worry too much.
Don't lose your control over things.
You can kiss me if you like,
You can pat my back,
tickle my belly or stroke my breasts
for a while, if it comforts you.
Sometimes it can be heavenly,
this licking the rim of the forbidden
frontiers of human life.

"That's what he wants, that's exactly
what he's looking for," a voice leered far off.
"But I have to go ultimately,
I've a man waiting at home for me."

"Maybe read a poem of yours,"
someone said. My heart raced wild
and I heard some girls gossip in the next room—
What if he gets sick in Europe?
Don't we get sick in Asia?
"Just take it easy," another voice echoed
"You won't go psychotic. Remember one thing,
whatever happens, you can always make a comeback."
Faces of my dear ones veered past my face.
I felt the delicate thread of my life
slipping through my fingers
  "Hey man, it's fine. Don't worry too much."
My host shouted. "Drink lots of water."
Drink black tea or coffee," a guest suggested.
"Or take lots of orange juice."

"Maybe sing your favorite song," a woman said.
"Or recite one of your Hindu mantras."
"Maybe stick your finger into your throat"
another voice came sheepishly, "And throw up.
You probably haven't digested everything yet."

Questions came like wind slaps.
"Can you tell me what they call *boredom*
in your mother tongue? Do you remember
your email account and password?
Discuss your children, if you have any.
Shall I bring my little daughter before you?
Maybe you'd feel better then,
seeing her brilliant eyes."

I imagined a child's face and clung to it,
like a penitent would hold onto
a sacred cow's tail in his afterlife,
and slept on it, all through the river of blood...

Hours passed by
and then I heard someone say—
What if he had freaked out?
What if Death had stalked our house tonight?

Hearing these words, I woke up
knowing I'd come back, stepped on
the familiar shores of life
where Death's feared, a distant distrustful thing.
My drowse burst like a glacial that cracks
from rumble of a seed of fire
that explodes somewhere in earth's deep sleep.

Celtic light: *Leslie Castle*

After a while
little flustered by my pagan adulation

she blushed,
her cheekbones blazed

like Annapurna summits
in the ruddy light of the morning sun,

her nose twitched
and she pleaded,

almost on
the edge of an accusation:

"If you won't stop
taking my photos,

I'd start
shining your shoes."

Her face glowed from
the shimmer of the tiny lake

slumbering outside
her castle window in the early hours of the night.

Inside, in the hushed
Edwardian silence lit by the aromatic candles

I imagined
a goddess bending onto

the steps of a rock mountain
shining syllables of nomadic winds

and bog lands
with her long tongue and warm breath

fermented from
Celtic coal buried beneath

weight of centuries of black sleep.

Look-alike, Galway

She held my book
like she would have cradled my baby

had we met and
married in early eighties

and sang songs
of the drifting winds that once visited

her frenzied dance
on the chest of naked glacial and sun parched continents.

Later in the bar as I stretched
folds of her skin back on her luscious face

years receded into
the dim drawers of my age,

time stepped down
the ladder of my lifespan,

a monkey-thief
in my youth's backyard.

Her long jawed-face
reminded me of Tara

or some rock goddess
as the dark pelt waters from distant bog lands

rushed through
my tumultuous frame.

The moist mouth
in her long Yeti face,

an Irish water well
I tried to see my tiger shadow in ...

"You look like a lover
I had in the Himalayas decades ago."

Silence

The moment I enter the Valley, nausea thrashes my well-being. A chill seeps into my bones and I close my eyes. Near Annapurna glacials, I had remained quite cosy, next to a warm hearth. Right away I regret my return to the slum of human destiny, ashtray of our shattered dreams.

At last I open my eyes to see Buddha's kingdom suffering like a snail. Where are the villages of huge brass bells? What fumes have filled the spacious squares of rituals? What vehicles have trampled fields of fragrance?

Overnight, a demon has sucked the fragrances of this once an exhilarating valley, leaving it deserted — wrinkled and crumpled sheet of a newspaper.

In a fraction of a second, its century of silences has been shattered eternally. Without a regret or guilt.

I open my eyes to enter this labyrinth of nightmares, nonplussed that the floral fields I celebrated in my dreams never actually existed.

I open my eyes to discover that the first casualty of this expansion— silence. A cadence of a melody I'd carried like a sacred song all these years, a nucleus of my waterwells. Has it been been unscrupulously misplaced and forgotten in the schemes of the cities?

Awestruck, I feel I'd remained at ease all these days and weeks when I was alone on the mule paths. But the moment I entered the city, I lost them all, syllables of the secret song that I hummed all these times.

It's in the cities that I've spent the saddest moments of my life.

Nirala Series

A Series of Contemporary Writing

Annapurna & Stains of Blood
Life, Travels & Writing on a Page of Snow
Yuyutsu R D Sharma
ISBN 81-8250-012-5 2008 Hard pp.200

Ocean in a Drop
Yoga, Meditation and Life in the Himalayas
Swami Chandresh
ISBN 81-8250- 005-2 2006 Hard pp.348

Tamang Shamans
An Ethnopsychiatric Study of Ecstasy and Healing in Nepal
Larry G. Peters
ISBN 81-8250-009-5 2007 Paper pp.179

Maoists in the Land of Buddha
An Analytical Study of the Maoist Insurgency in Nepal
Prakash A. Raj
ISBN 81-85693-42-0 2004 Hard pp.210

The Yeti
Spirit of Himalayan Forest Shamans
Larry G. Peters
ISBN 81-85693-57-9 2004 Hard pp.128

Rana Rule in Nepal
Shaphalya Amatya
ISBN 81-85693-67-6 2004 Hard pp.408

Trance, Initiation & Psychotherapy in Nepalese Shamanism
Essays on Tamang and Tibetian Shamanism
Larry G.Peters
ISBN 81-85693-79-X 2004 Hard pp.412

Folk Tales of Sherpa and Yeti
Collected by **Shiva Dhakal**
Adapted by **Yuyutsu RD Sharma**
ISBN 81-8250-002-0 2008 Paper pp.125

The Gurkha Connection
A History of Gurkha Recruitment in the British Army
Purushottam Baskota
ISBN 81-85693-77-3 2007 Paper pp.221

Dolpo :The Hidden Paradise
A Journey to the Endangered Sanctuary of the Himalayan Kingdom of Nepal
Karna Sakya
ISBN 81-85693-73-0 2006 Paper pp.246

Malla Coins of Medieval Nepal
Jagdish Chandra Regmi
ISBN 81-85693-60-9 2008 Hard

The Dhimals: Miraculous Migrants of Himal
An Anthropological Study of a Nepalese Ethnic Group
Rishikeshab Raj Regmi
ISBN 81-8250-008-7 2008 Paper pp.269

The Questions of Dharma in the Mahabhatara
Birendra Mishra
ISBN 81-85693-48-X 2008 Hard pp.226

The Gurungs: Thunder of Himal
A Cross-Cultural Study of a Nepalese Ethnic Group
Murari P. Regmi
ISBN 81-85693-49-8 2002 Paper pp.238

The Gurkhas
A History of the Recruitment in the British Indian Army
Kamal Raj Singh Rathaur
ISBN 81-85693-85-4 2000 Paper pp.128

The Political Economy of Land, Landlessness and
Migration in Nepal
Nanda R. Shrestha
ISBN 81-85693-87-0 2001 Hard pp.309

Tourism in Nepal
Marketing Challenges
Hari Prasad Shrestha
ISBN 81-85693-69-2 2000 Hard pp.399

Ethnic Conflict in Bhutan
Political and Economic Dimensions
Mathew Joseph C.
ISBN 81-85693-68-4 1999 Hard pp.251

Mountain Dimensions
An Altitude Geographic Analysis of Environment and
Development of the Himalayas
Ram Kumar Pandey
ISBN 81-85693-43-9 1999 pp.260 Hard

Wildlife in Nepal
Rishikesh Shaha & Richard M. Mitchell
With Color Plates by Nanda Shumsher J.B. Rana
ISBN 81-85693-31-5 2001 Paper pp.142

Nepal: Missing Elements in the Development Thinking
Gunanidhi Sharma
ISBN 81-85693-66-8 2000 Hard pp.282

Art and Culture of Nepal
An Attempt towards Preservation
Saphalya Amatya
ISBN 81-85693-63-3 1999 Hard pp.282

Popular Deities, Emblems and Images of Nepal
Dhruba K Deep
ISBN 81-85693-39-0 2003 pp.180

Vishwarupa Mandir
A Study of Changu Narayan, Nepal's most Ancient Temple
Jeff Lidke
ISBN 81-85693-59-3 1996 Hard pp.213

Religious Minorities in Nepal
*An Analysis of the State of the Buddhists and
Muslims in the Himalayan Kingdom*
Mollica Dostider
ISBN 81-85693-47-1 1996 Hard pp.213

Human Rights in the Hindu Buddhist Traditions
Lal Deosa Rai
ISBN 81-85693-46-3 1995 Hard pp 188

Fire of Himal
An Anthropological Study of Sherpas of Nepal Himalayan Region
ISBN 81-85693-64-1 1999 Paper pp.314

The Khasa Kingdom
A Trans- Himalayan Empire of the Middle Ages
Surya Mani Adhikary
ISBN 81-85693-50-1 Paper 1997 pp.215

Hindu-Buddhist Festival of Nepal
Hemant Kumar Jha
ISBN 81-85693-40-4 1996 Hard pp.117

**Nepal: A Concise History of
the Cultural Scenario of the Himalayan Kingdom**
Jagdish Shumsher Rana
ISBN 81-85693-45-5 Hard 1995 pp.120

Bhutan : A Movement in Exile
D.N.S. Dhakal & Christopher Strawn
ISBN 81-8250-001-2 Paper 2007 pp.639

Encounter Wildlife in Nepal
Karna Sakya
ISBN 81-85693-38-2 Hard 1996 pp.296

Nepal-India
Democracy in the Making of Mutual Trust
Dinesh Bhattarai & Pradip Khatiwada
ISBN 81-85693-36-6 1993 Hard pp.324

Politics of the Himalayan River Waters
An Analysis of the River Water Issues of Nepal, India and Bangladesh
B. C. Uprety
ISBN 81-85693-32-3 Hard 1993 pp.228

The Himalayan Mind
A Cross-Cultural Nepalese Investigation
Murari P. Regmi
ISBN 81-85693-29-3 Hard 1993 pp.240

Kathmandu, Patan & Bhaktapaur
An Archaeological Anthropology of
the Royal Cities of the Kathmandu Valley
Rishikeshab R. Regmi
ISBN 81-85693-30-7 Hard 1997 pp.111

A Glossary of Himalayan Buddhism
Jagdish Chandra. Regmi
ISBN 81-85693-28-5 Hard 1994 pp.212

The Nepala-Mahatmya
Legends on the Sacred Places and Deities of Nepal
Jayaraj Acharya
ISBN 81-85693-27-7 Hard 1992 pp.320

Cultural Heritage of Nepal Terai
Ram Dayal Rakesh
ISBN 81-85693-26-9 Hard 1994 pp.240

The Nepali Congress
An Analysis of the Party's Performance
in the General Elections and its Aftermath
B.C.Uprety
ISBN 81-85693-33-1 Hard 1993 pp.203

Recent Nepal
An Analysis of the Recent Democratic Upsurge and its Aftermath
Laksman Bahadur K.C.
ISBN 81-85693-24-2 Hard 1993 pp.242

Folktales of Mithila
Ram Dayal Rakesh
ISBN 81-85693-55-2 Hard 1996 pp.126

Secrets of Shangri-la
An Inquiry into the Lore, Legend and Culture of Nepal
Nagendra Sharma
ISBN 81-85693-18-8 Hard 1992 pp.292

Gods and Mountains
The Folk Culture of the Himalayan Kingdom of Nepal
Kesar Lal
ISBN 81-85693-12-9 Hard 1993 pp.176

Making of Modern Nepal
A Study of History, Art and Culture of the Principalities of Western Nepal
Ram Niwas Pandey
ISBN 81-85693-37-4 1997 Hard pp.816

Politics and Development in Nepal:
Some Issues
Narayan Khadka
ISBN 81-85693-21-8 1994 Hard pp.477

Indo-Nepal Trade Relations
A Historical Analysis of Nepal's Trade with the British India
Shri Ram Upadhyaya
ISBN 81-85693-20-X 1992 pp.287

Secrets of Shangri-La
An Inquiry into the Lore, Legend and Culture of Nepal
Nagendra Sharma
ISBN 81-85693-18-8   1992 pp.292

The Taming of Tibet
A Historical Account of Compromise and Confrontation
in Nepal-Tibet Relations (1900-1930)
Tirtha Prasad Mishra
ISBN 81-85693-16-1 1991 pp.324

Glimpses of Tourism, Airlines and Management in Nepal
B.R. Singh
ISBN 81-85693-15-3 1991   pp.128

Sales Promotion in Nepal
Policies and Practices
Parashar Prasad Koirala
ISBN 81-85693-14-5 1991 pp.196

Hindu-Buddhist Festival of Nepal
Hemant Kumar Jha
ISBN 81-85693-40-4   1996   Hard pp.117

Transit of Land Locked Countries and Nepal
Gajendra Mani Pradhan
ISBN 81-85693-08-0 1990 pp.240

Fundamentals of Library and Information Science
A Nepalese Response
Madhusudan Sharma Subedi
ISBN 81-85693-07-4 1990   pp.229

Folk Culture of Nepal
An Analytical Study
Ram Dayal Rakesh
ISBN 81-85693-06-4   1990 Hard pp.129

A Macro-economic Study of the Nepalese Plan Performance
Gunanidhi Sharma
ISBN 81-85693-06-4   1989   pp.129

Sources of Inflation in Asia
Theory and Evidences
Raghab D. Pant
ISBN 81-85693-03-X   1988 Hard pp.118

New Directions in Nepal- India Relations
Rishikesh Shaha
ISBN 81-85693-53-6   1995 Paper pp.59

IN NEPALI LANGUAGE
Panaharu Khalichan : Kavitaka Dui Dashak (Poems)
Yuyustu R.D. Sharma
ISBN 81-8250-004-4   2008 Paper pp. 102

Pashushala   (Animal Farm) (A Novel)
Georege Orwell
Translated from the English by Bijuli Prasad Kayast
ISBN 81-8250-000-1   2004 Paper pp.96

Nepalko Prajatantrik Andolan Ko Itihas
Surya Mani Adhikary
ISBN 81-85693-54-4   1998 Paper pp.468

Geetajanjali (Nepali)
Rabindra Nath Tagore
Translated from the Bengali by **Ramesh Bhatta & Pashupati Neopane**
ISBN 81-85693-83-8 2000 Paper pp.125

Sarpahoru Geet Sundainan
Pomes by **Shailendra Sakar**
ISBN 81-85693-97-8 1991 Hard pp.108

Nirala Series

A Series of Contemporary Literature

Annapurna Poems
Yuyutsu R D Sharma
ISBN 81-8250-013-5 2008 Hard pp.150

After Tagore
Poems Inspired by **Rabindranath Tagore**
David Ray
ISBN 81-8250-007-9 2008 Hard pp. 128

Kathmandu
Poems Selected and New (An English/Nepali Bilingual Edition)
Cathal O Searcaigh
Translated from the Gaelic by **Seamus Heaney,**
John Montague and others
Translated into the Nepali by *Yuyutsu R.D. Sharma*
ISBN 81-8250-006-0   2006 Hard pp. 105

The Lake Fewa & a Horse
Poems New
Yuyutsu R.D. Sharma
iSBN 81-8250-015-X 2008 Paper pp. 108

Muna Madan
A Play in the Jhyaure Folk Tradition
Laxmi P. Devkota
Translated from the Nepali by **Anand P. Shrestha**
ISBN 81-8250-014-1 2007 pp.65

Fever (Short Stories)
Sita Pandey
Translated from the Nepali
ISBN 81-85693-93-5 2001 Paper pp.96

Says Meera
An Anthology of Devotional Songs of Meera, India's Greatest Woman Poet
Translated from the Hindi by **Vijay Munshi**
ISBN 81-85693-96-X 2001 Paper pp.76

Some Female Yeti & other Poems
Yuyutsu R.D.
ISBN 81-8250-010-9 2008 pp.68

In the City of Partridges (Poems)
Jagdish Chatturvedi
ISBN 81-85693-99-4 2004 Paper pp.90

Roaring Recitals: Five Nepali Poets
Gopal Prasad Rimal, Bhupi Sherchan, Shailendra & Others
Translated from the Nepali by
Yuyutsu R.D. Sharma
ISBN 81-85693-95-1 1999 Hard pp.99